AUSTRALIAN ANIMALS

ADULT COLORING BOOK

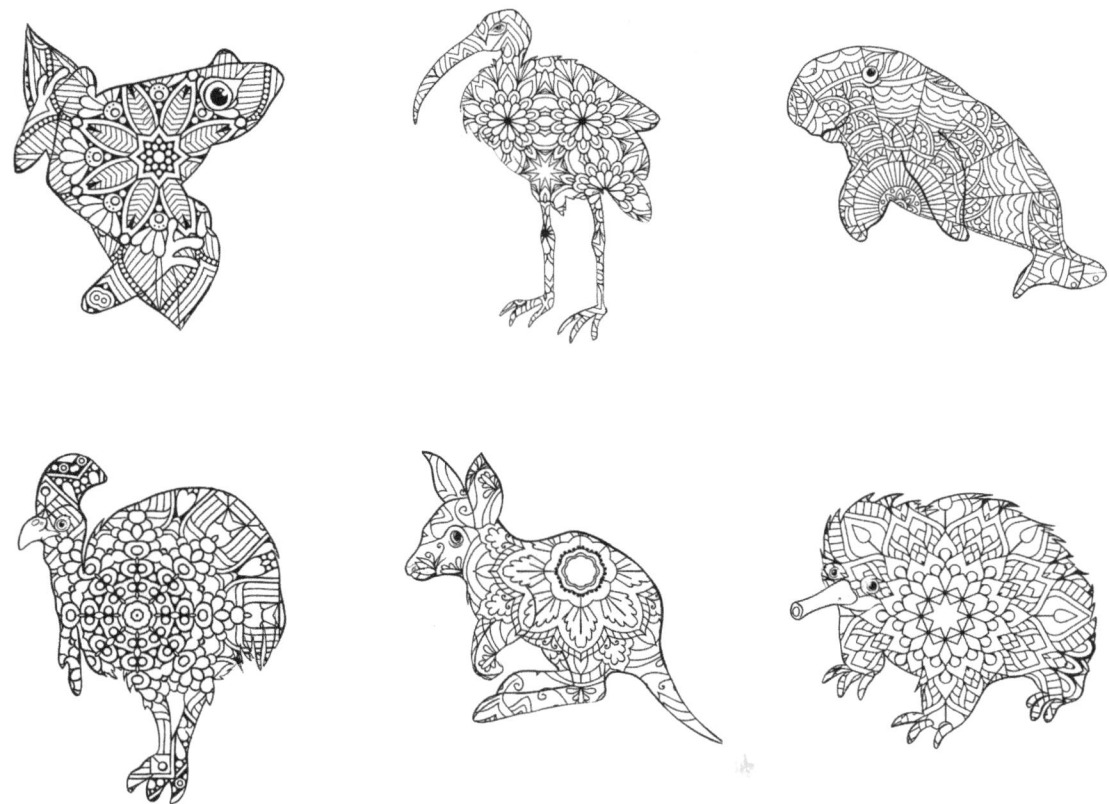

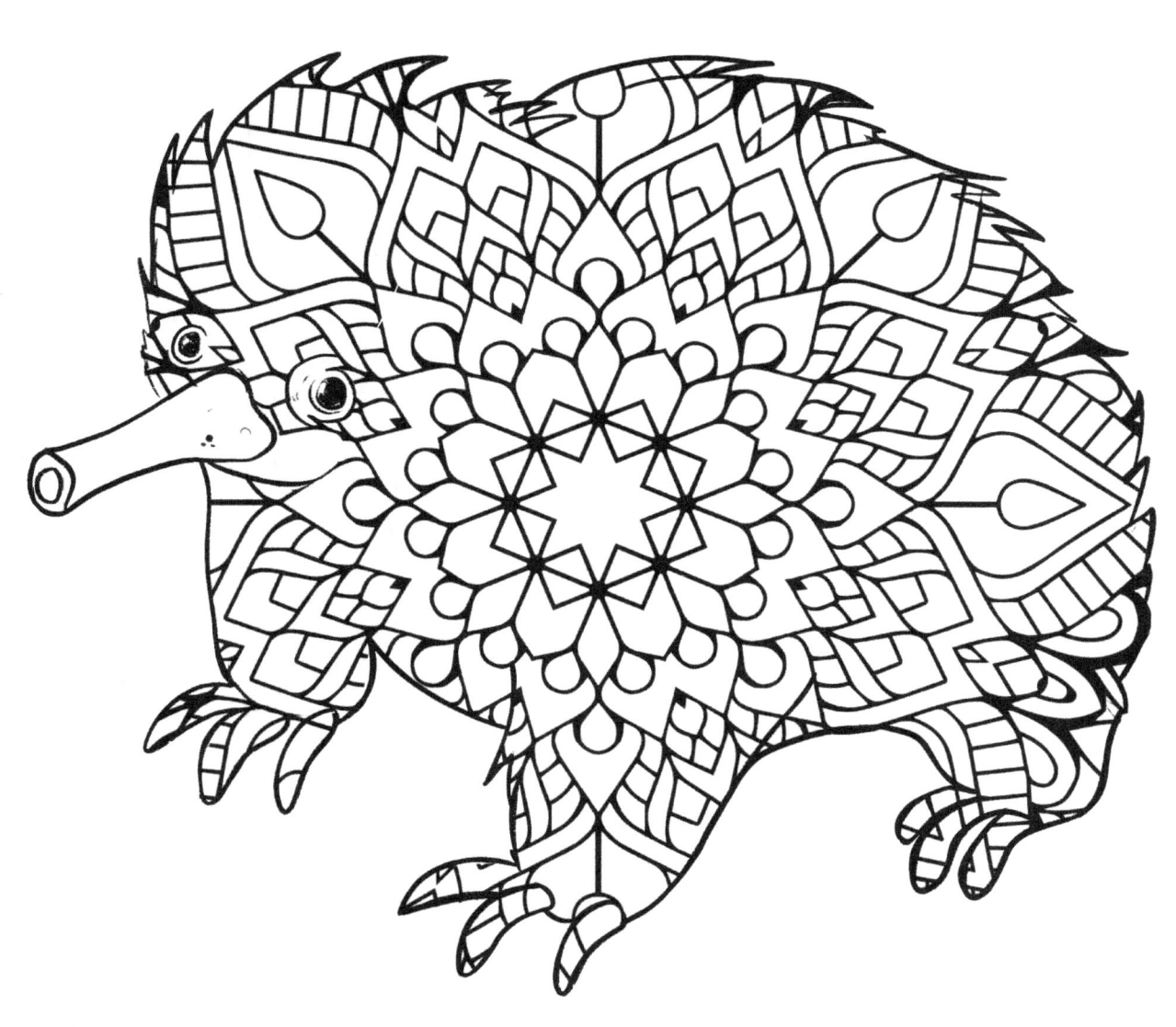

Echidna

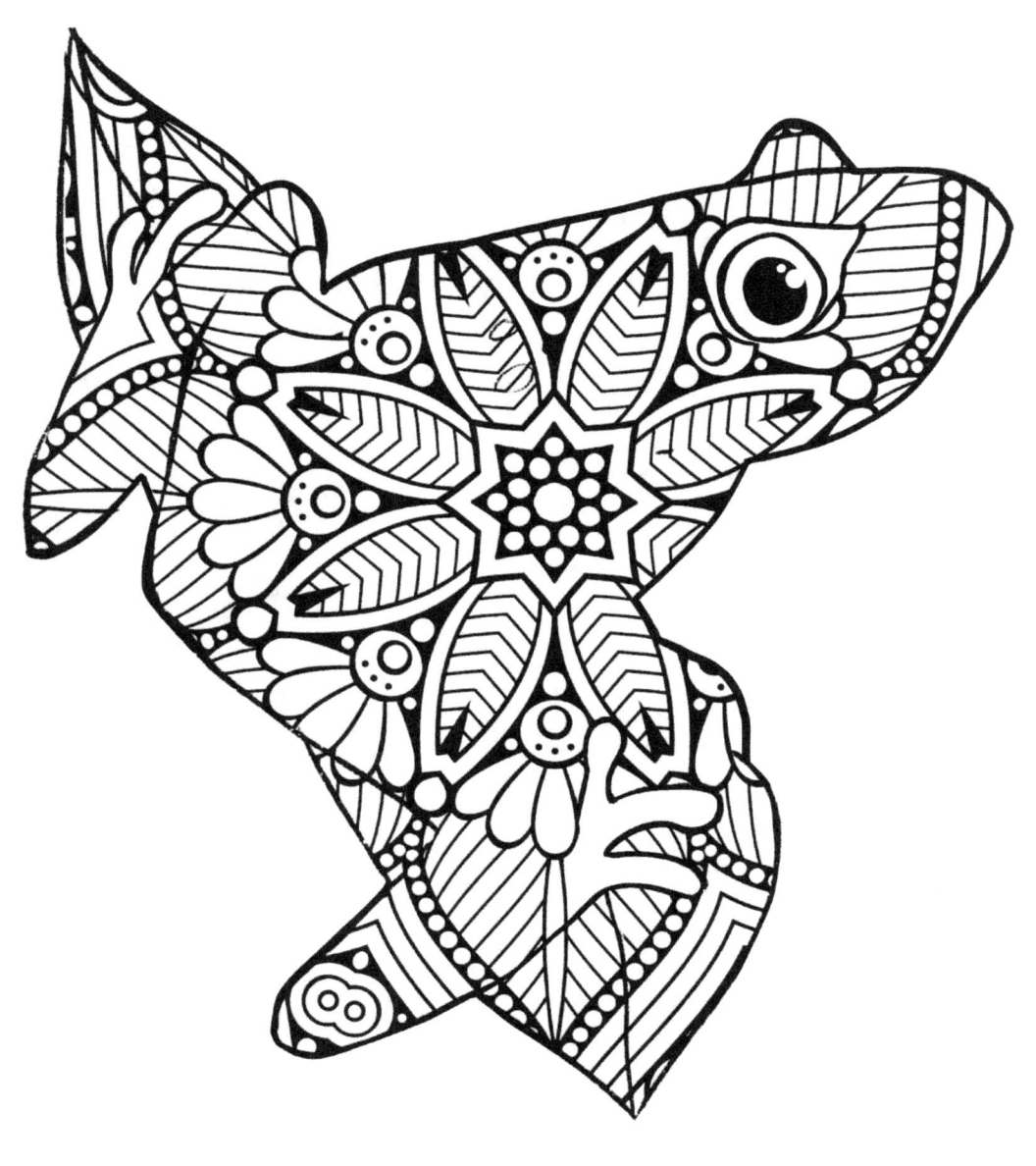

Javelin Frog

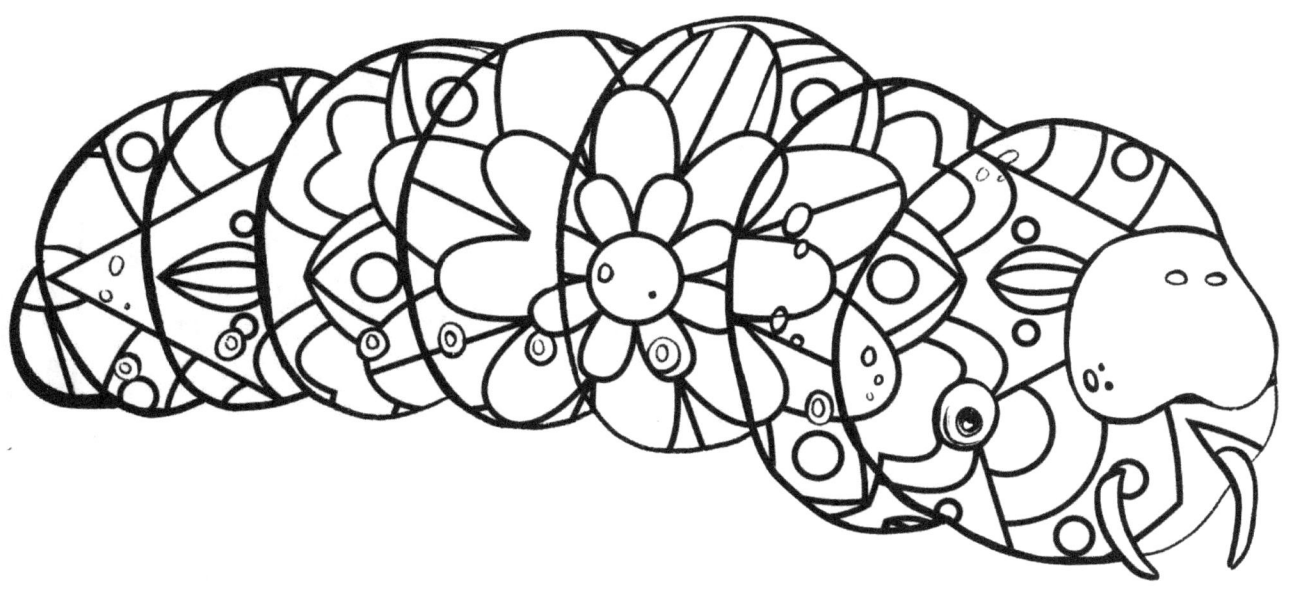

Witchetty Grub

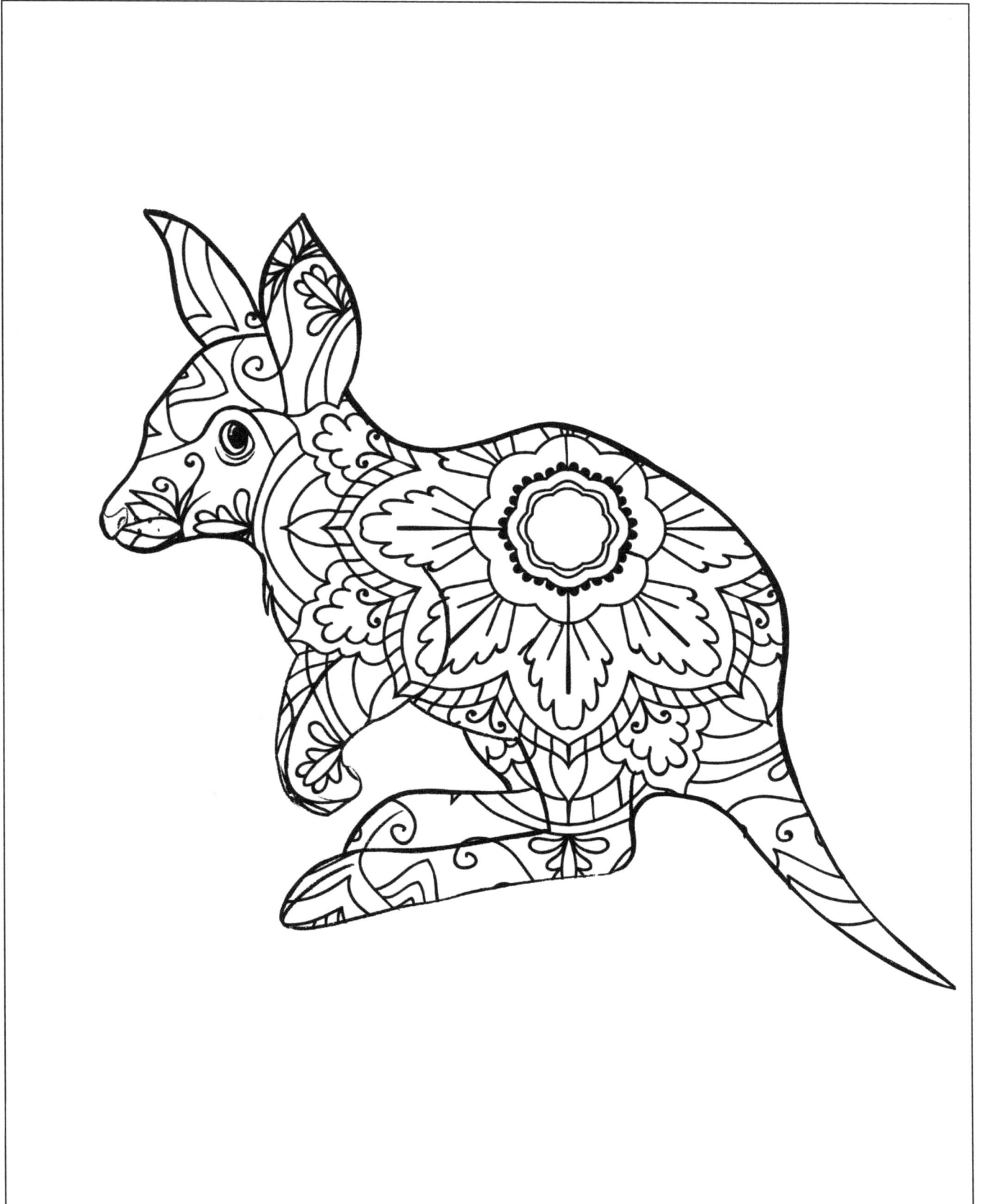

Wallaby

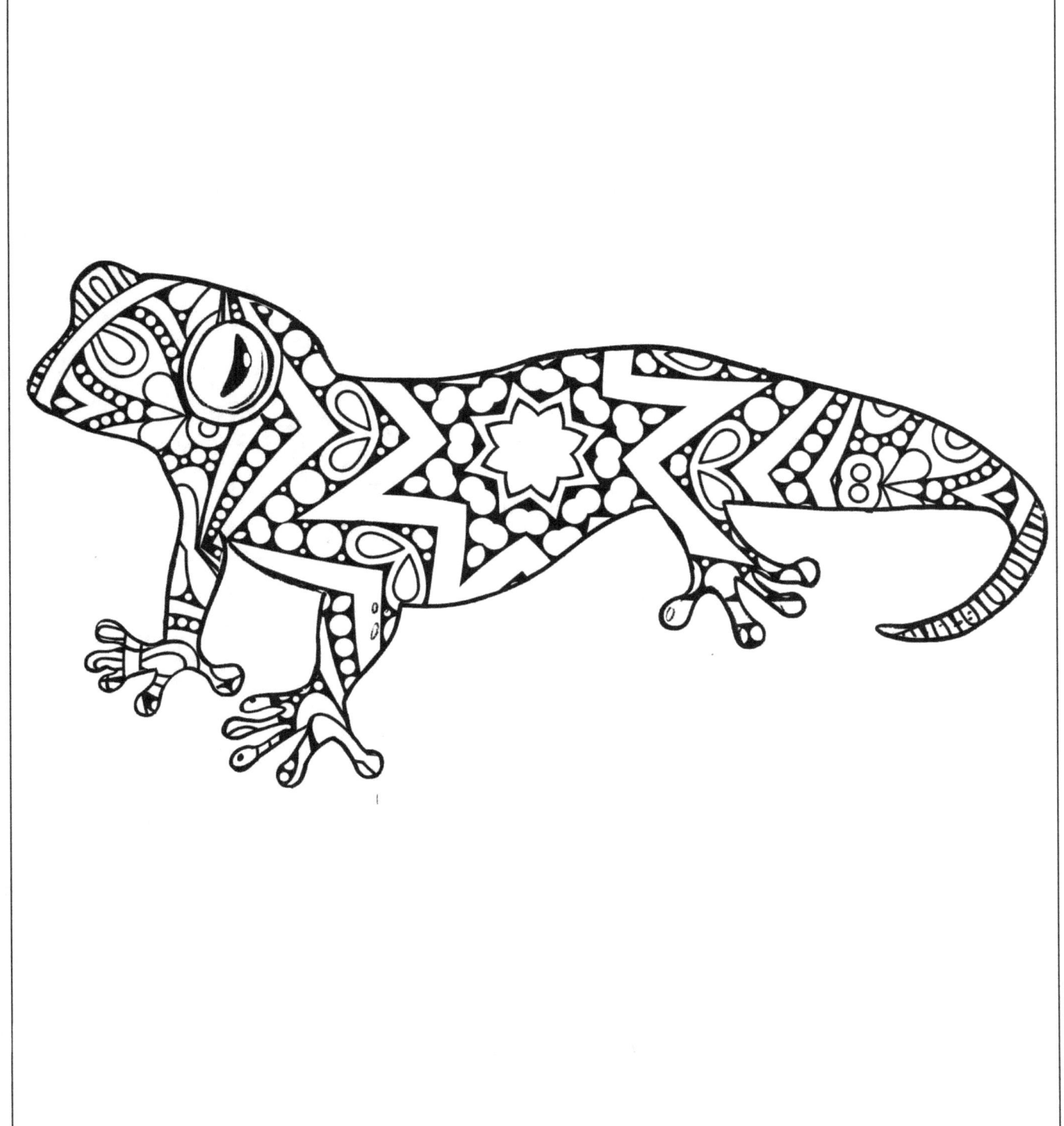

Velvet Gecko

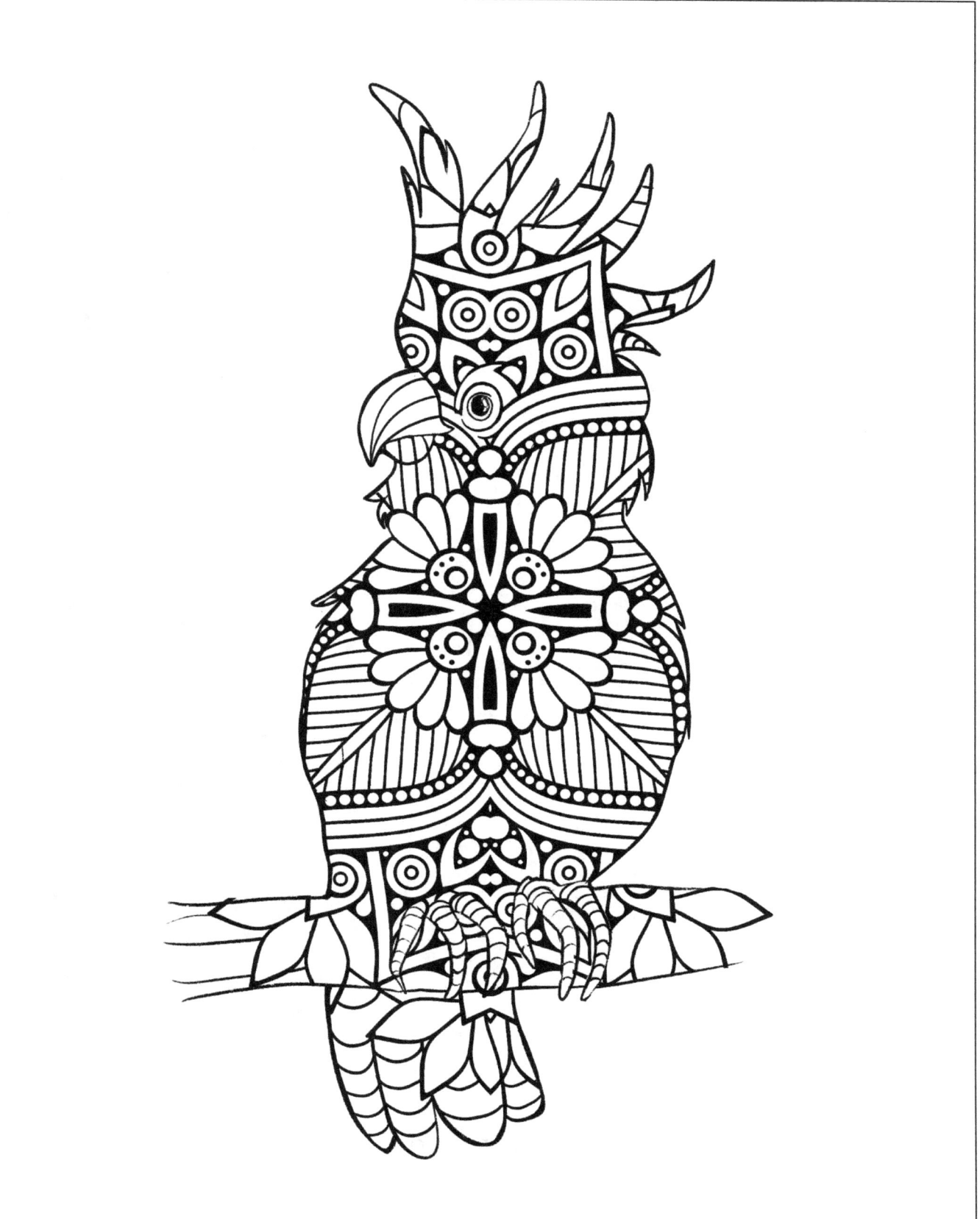

Cockatoo

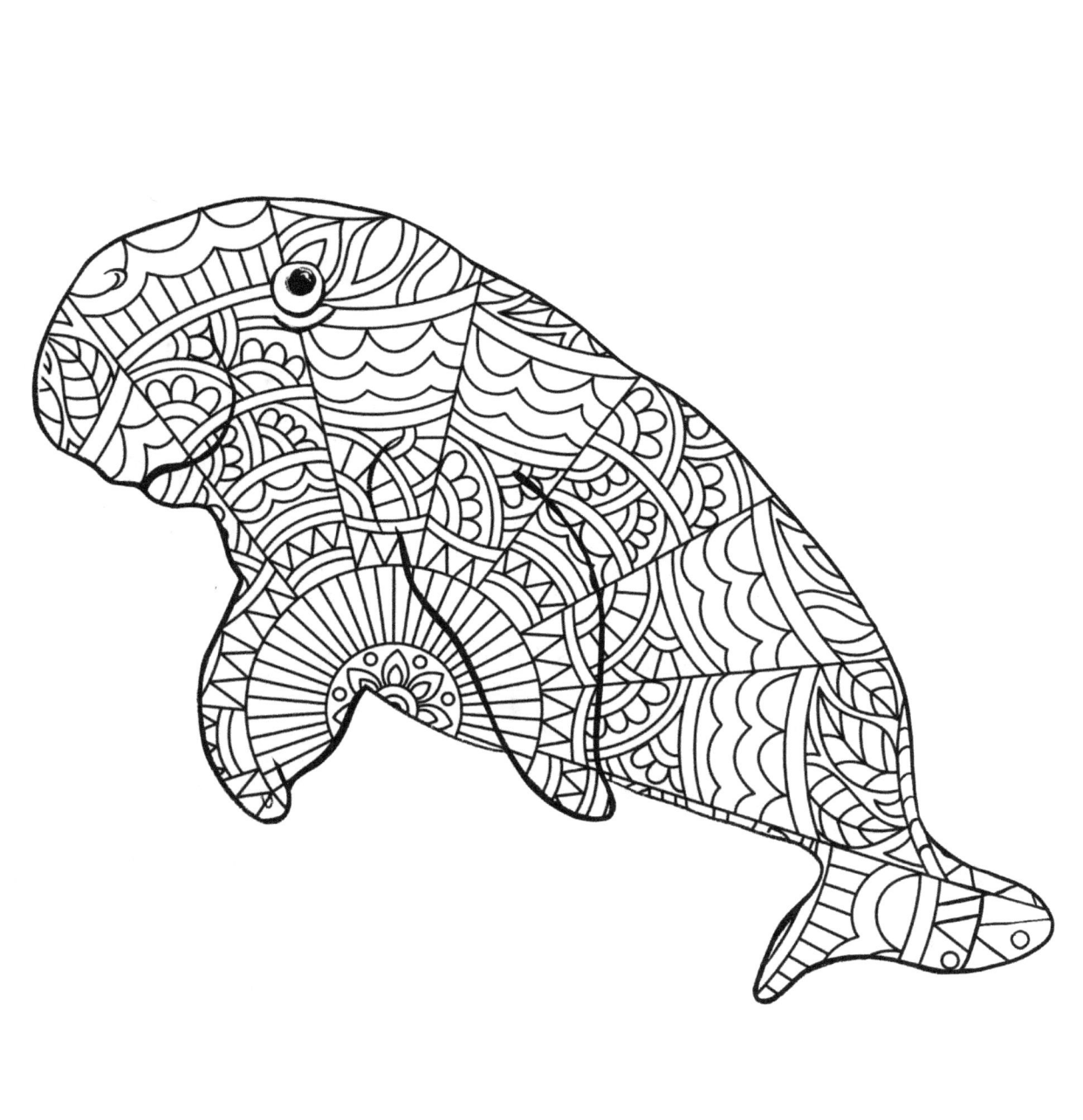

Dugong

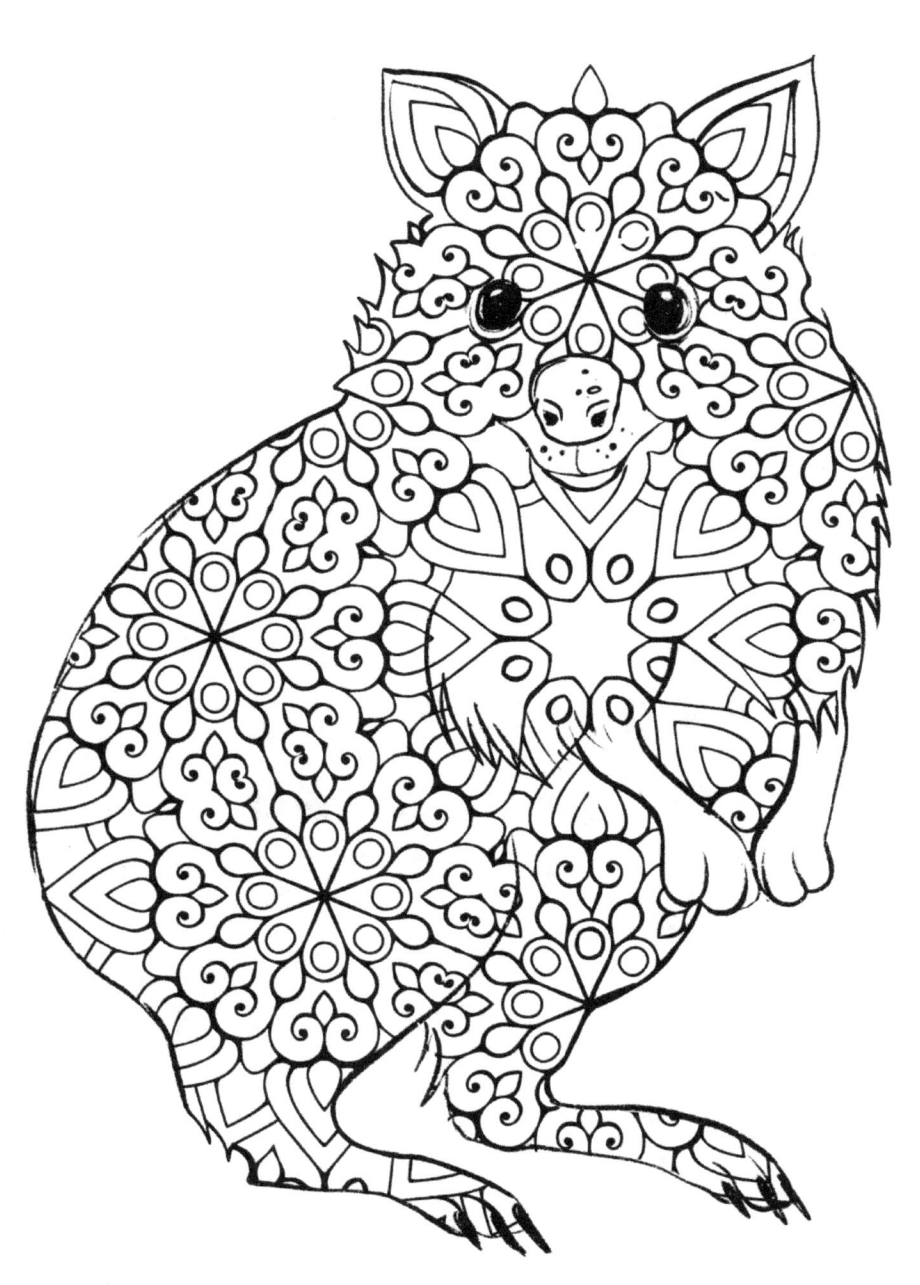

Quokka

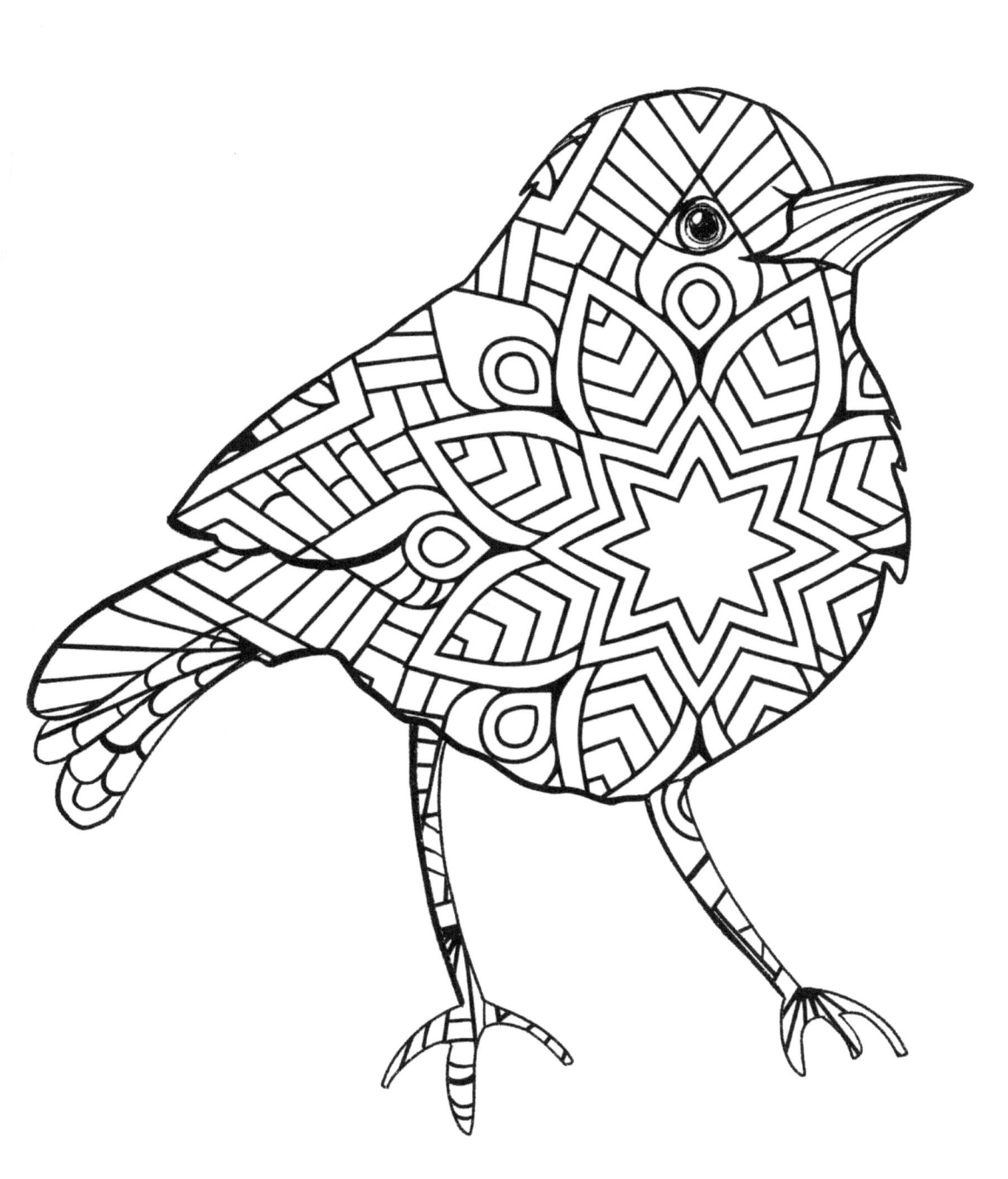

Origma

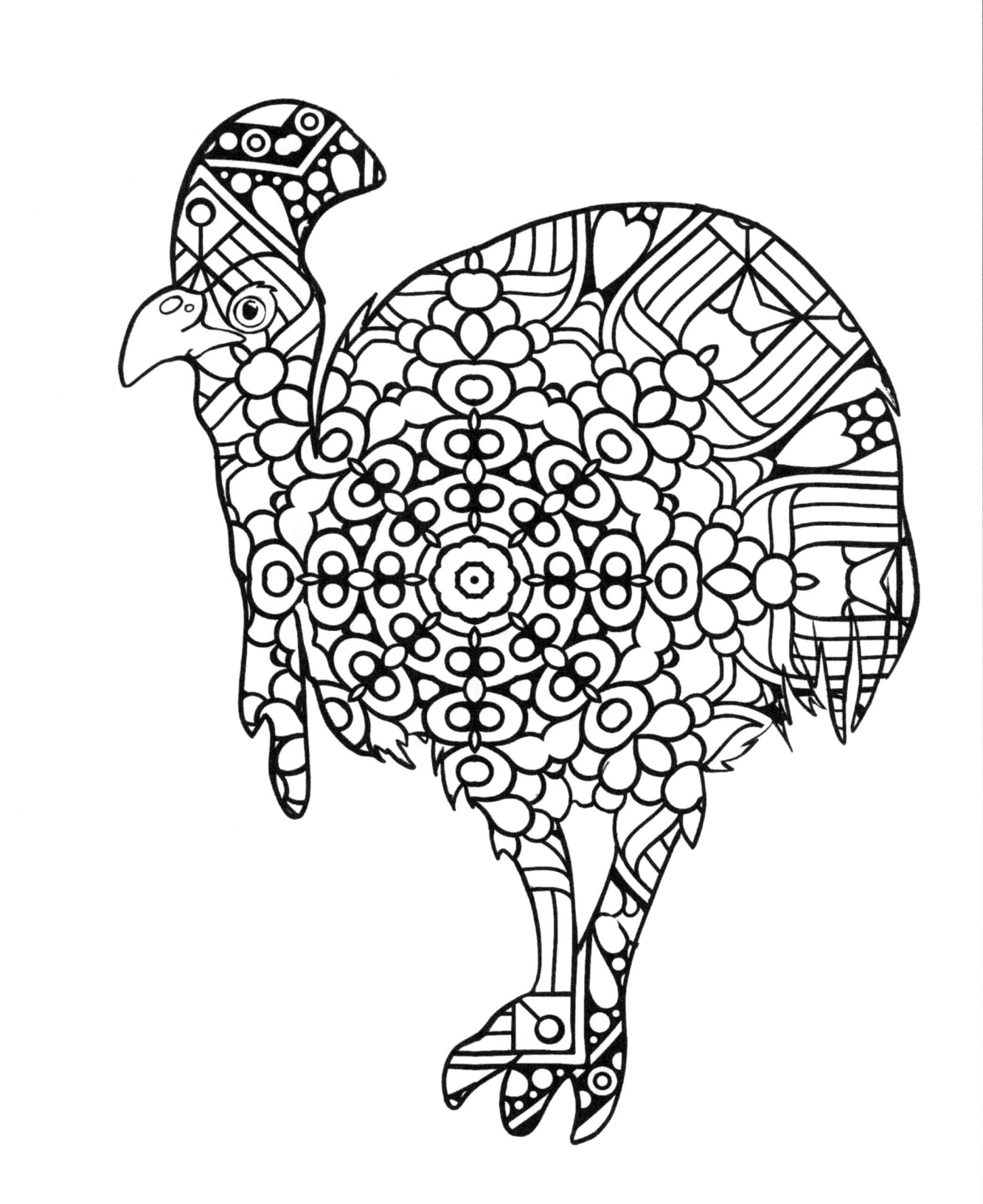

Ca

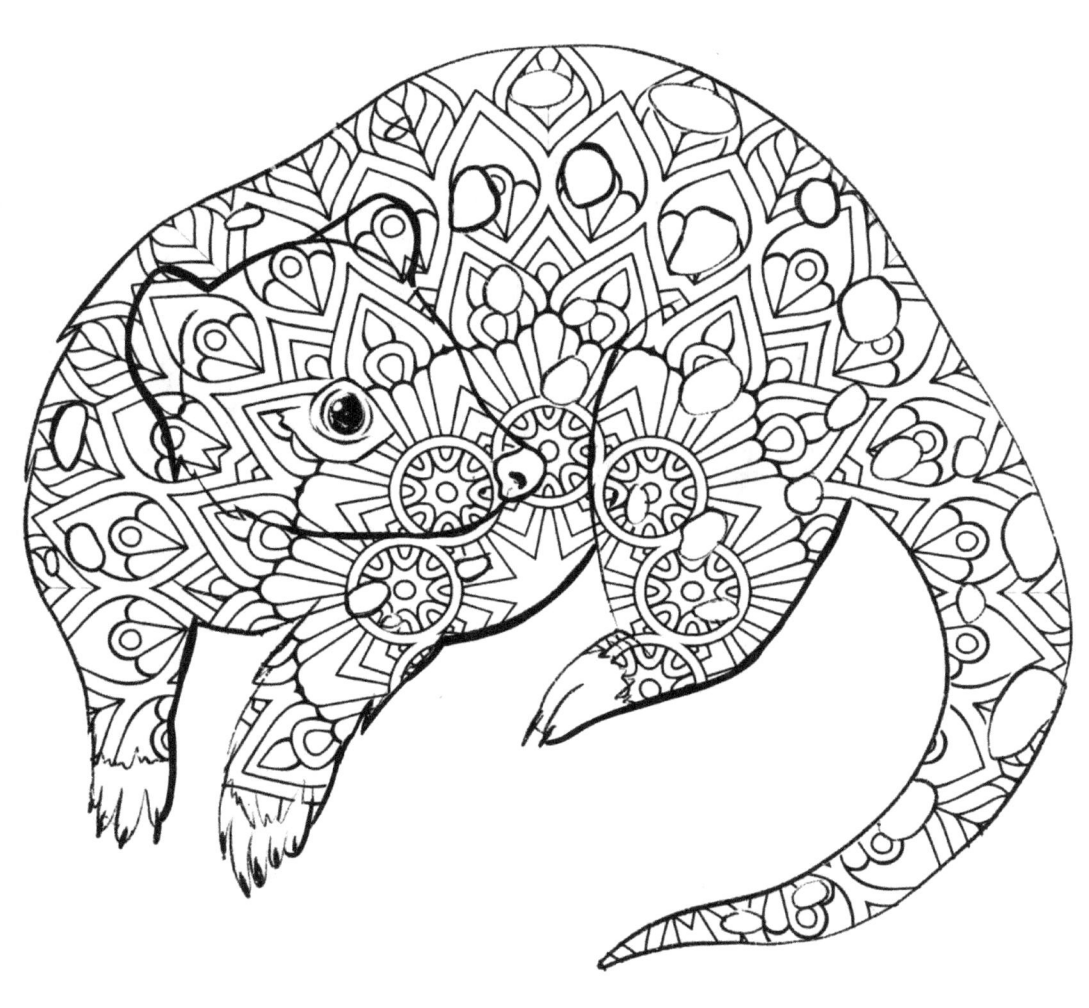

Quoll

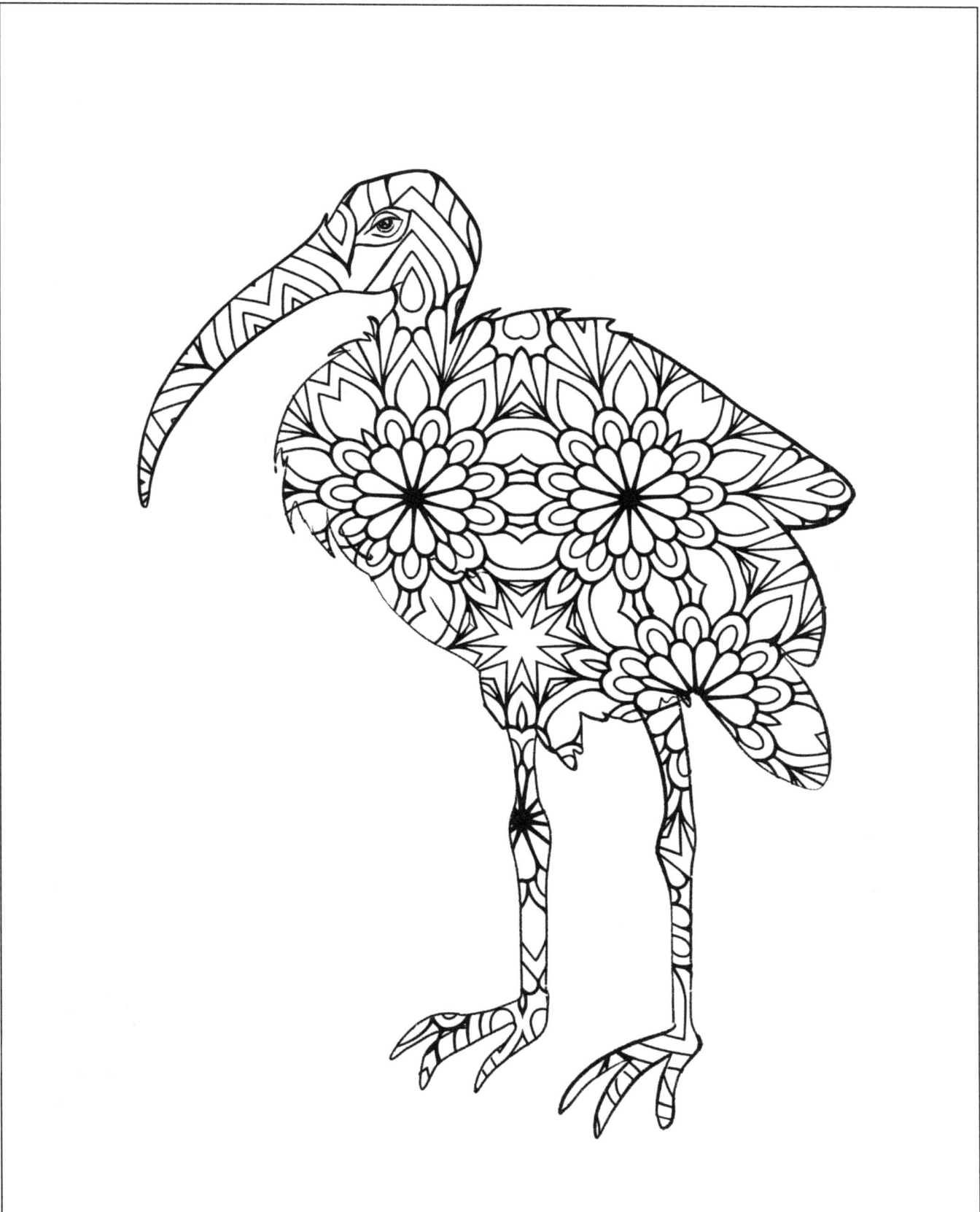

Ibis

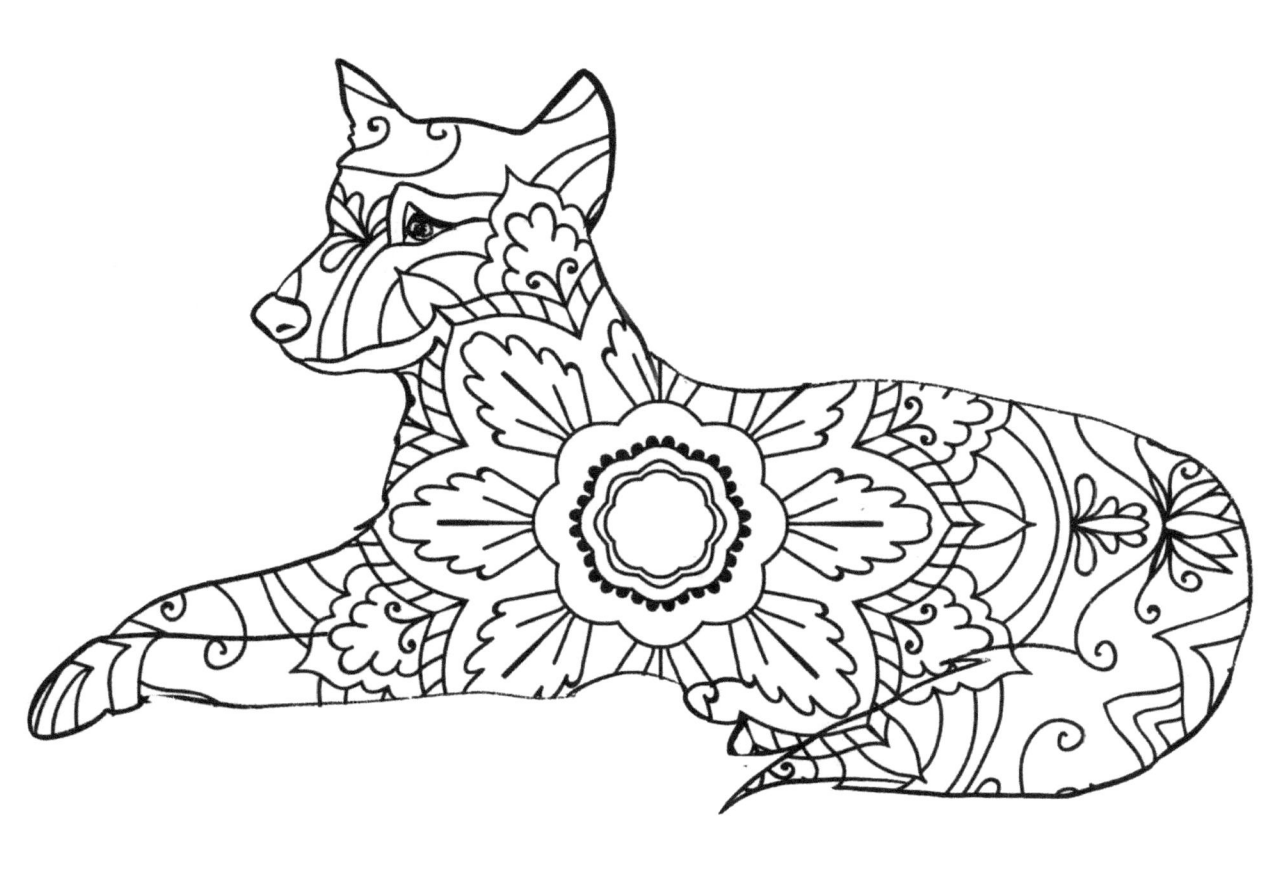

Dingo

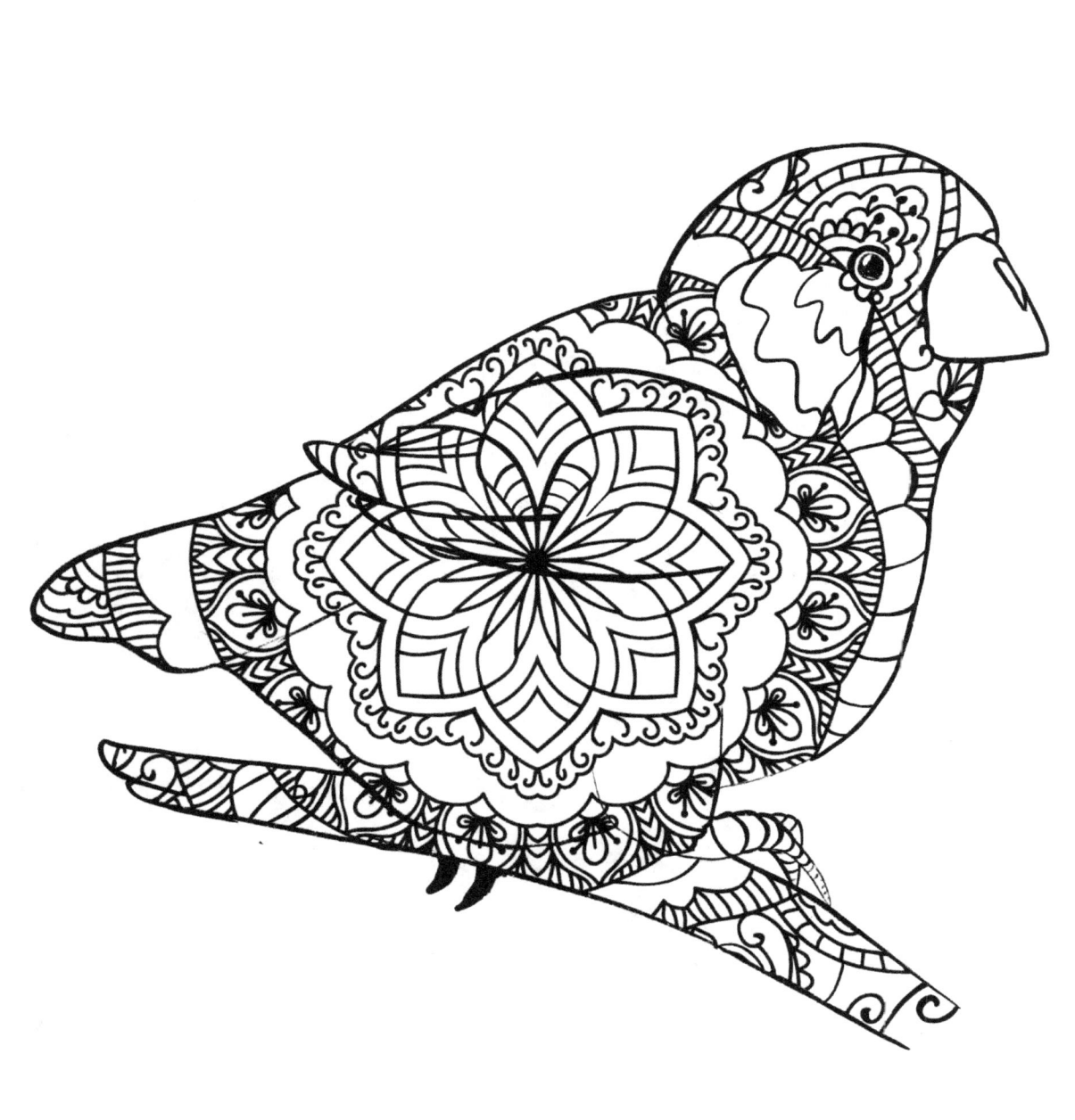

Zebra Finch

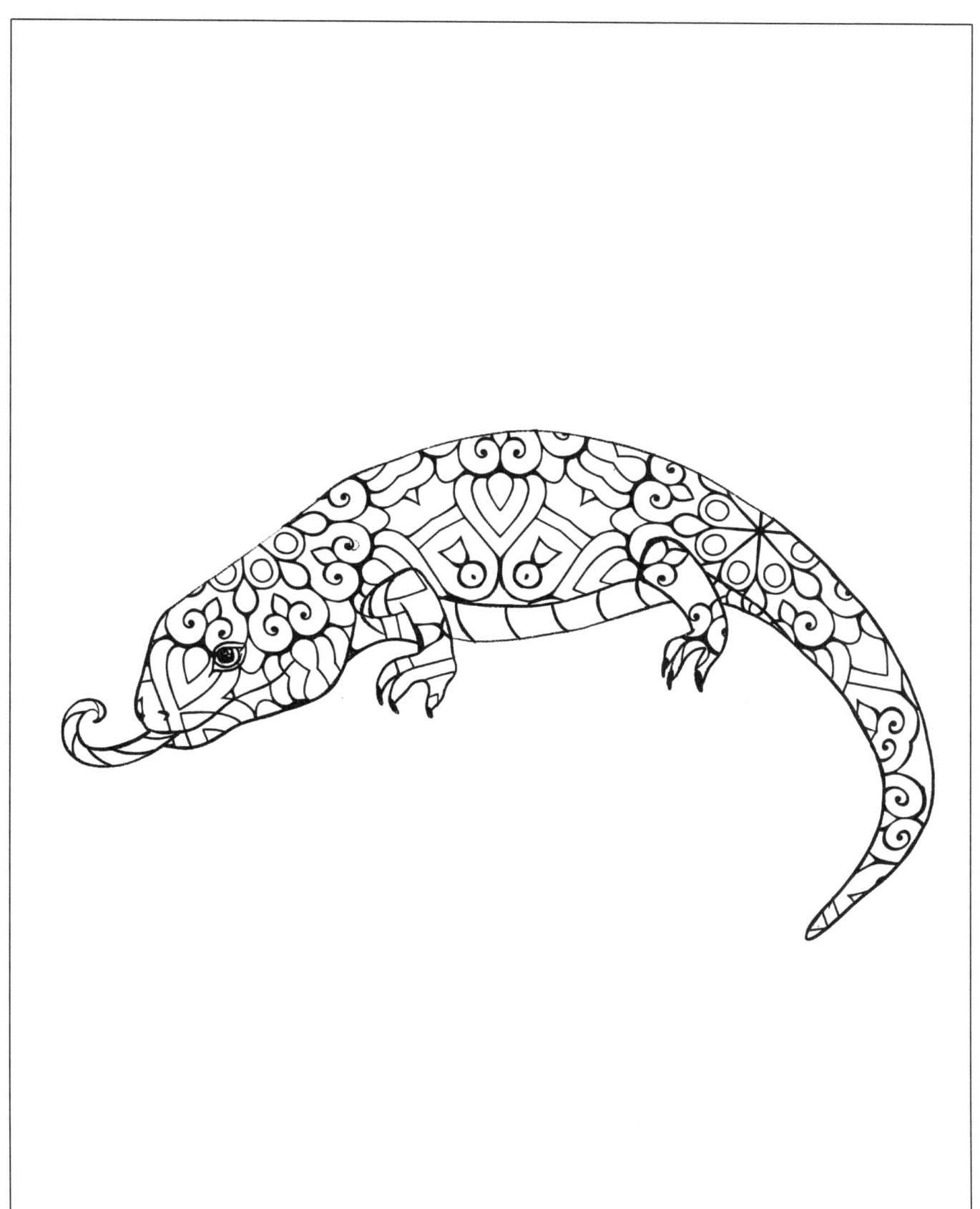

Blue Tongue Skink

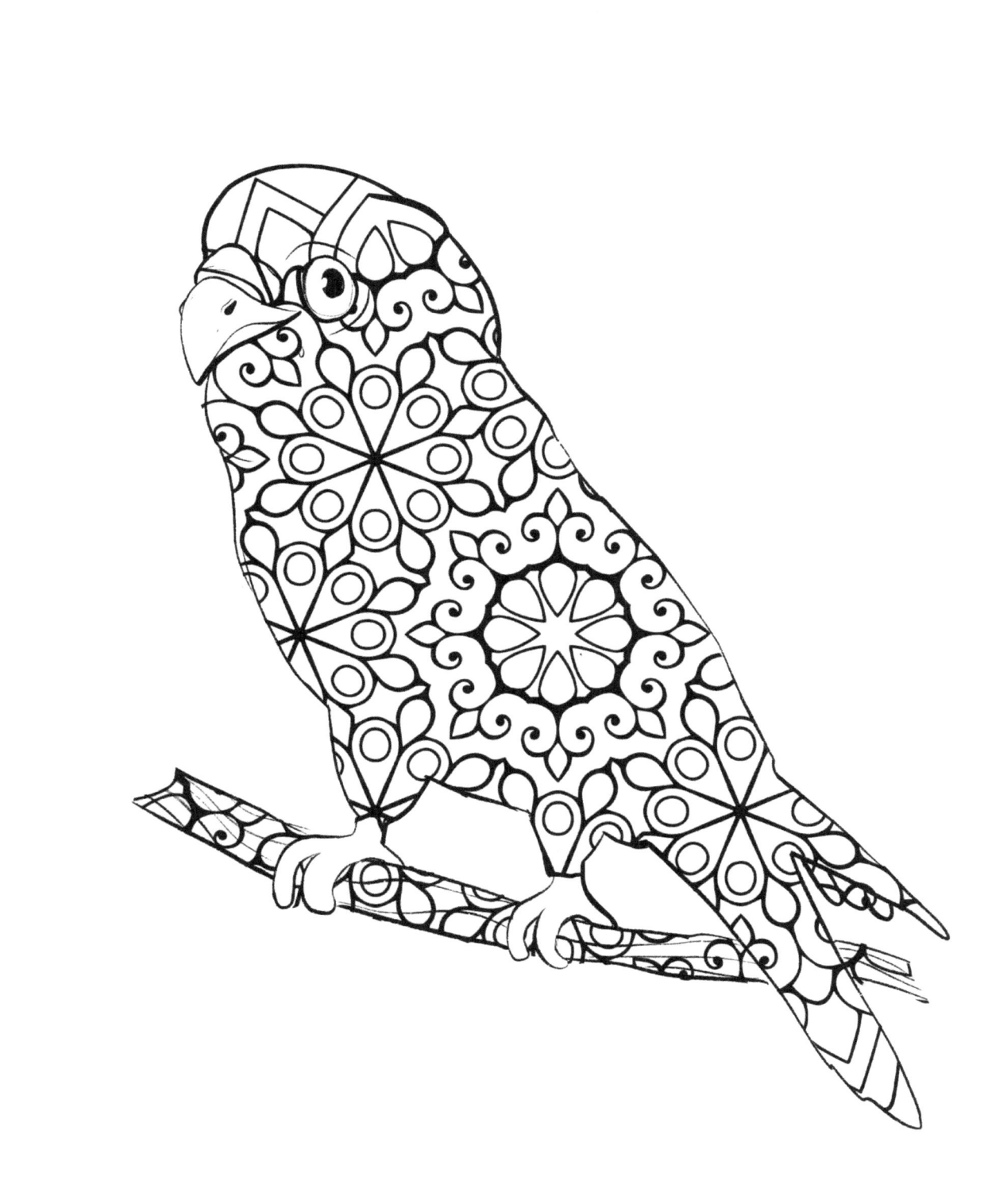

Budgerigar

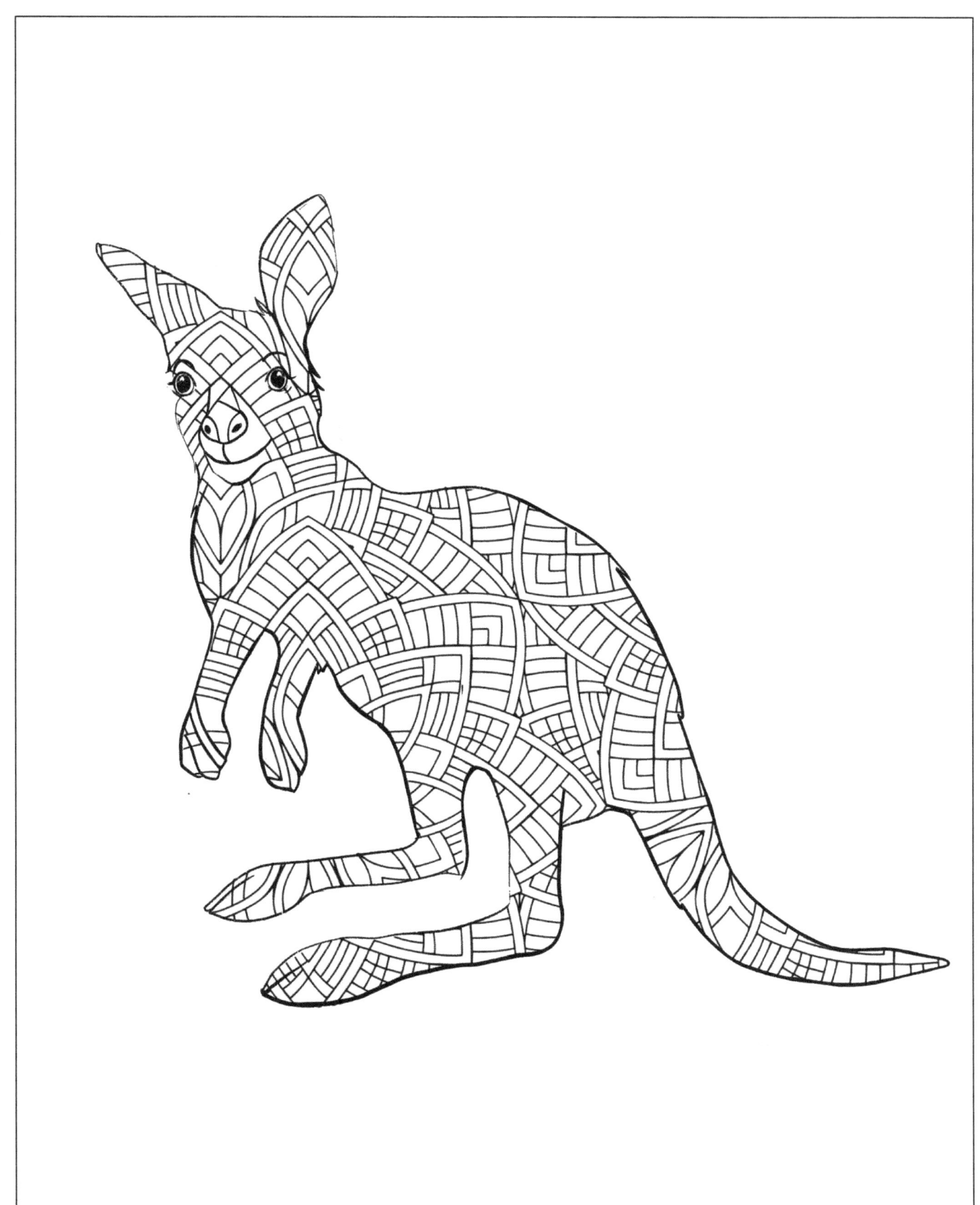

Kangaroo

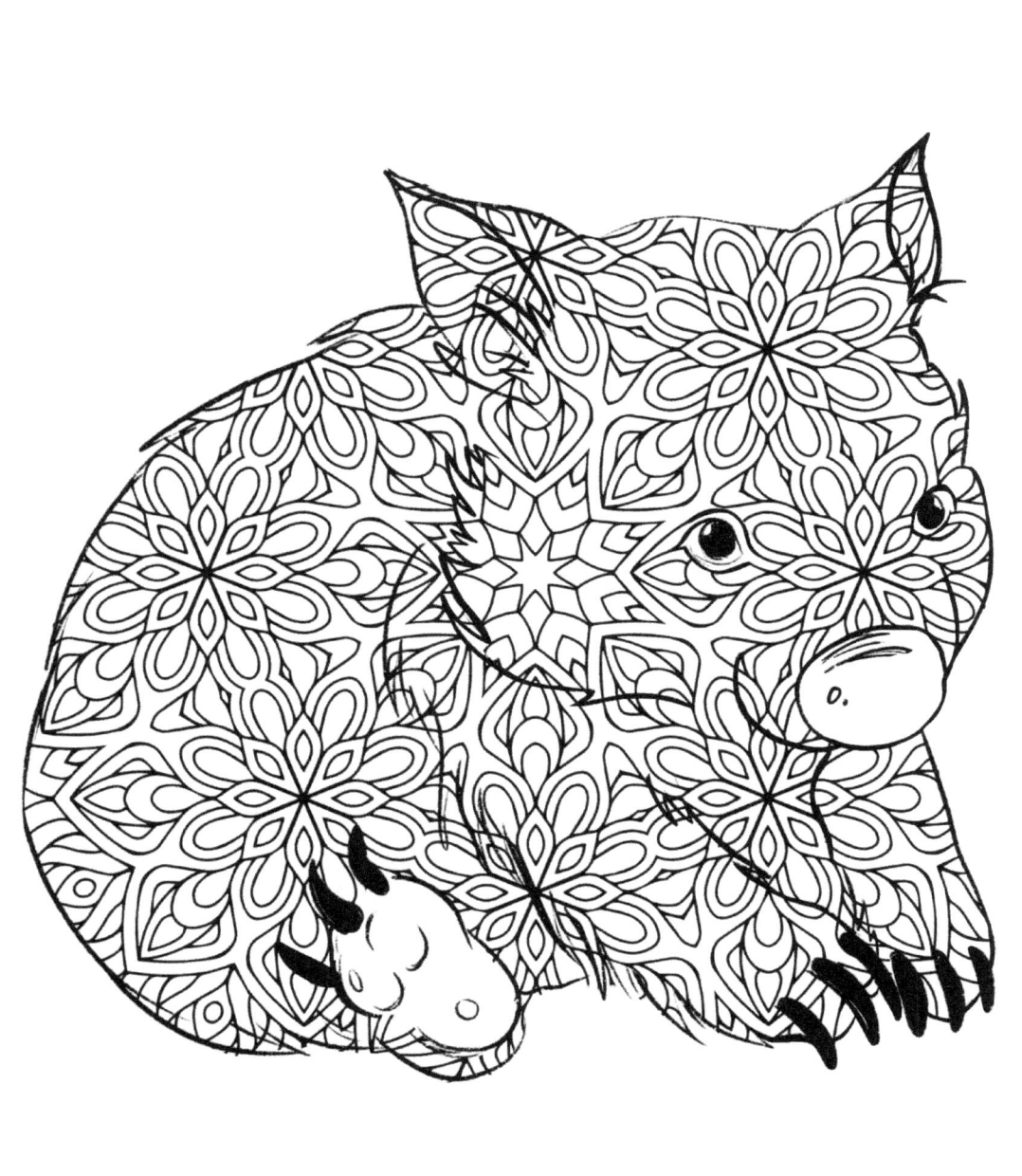

Wombat

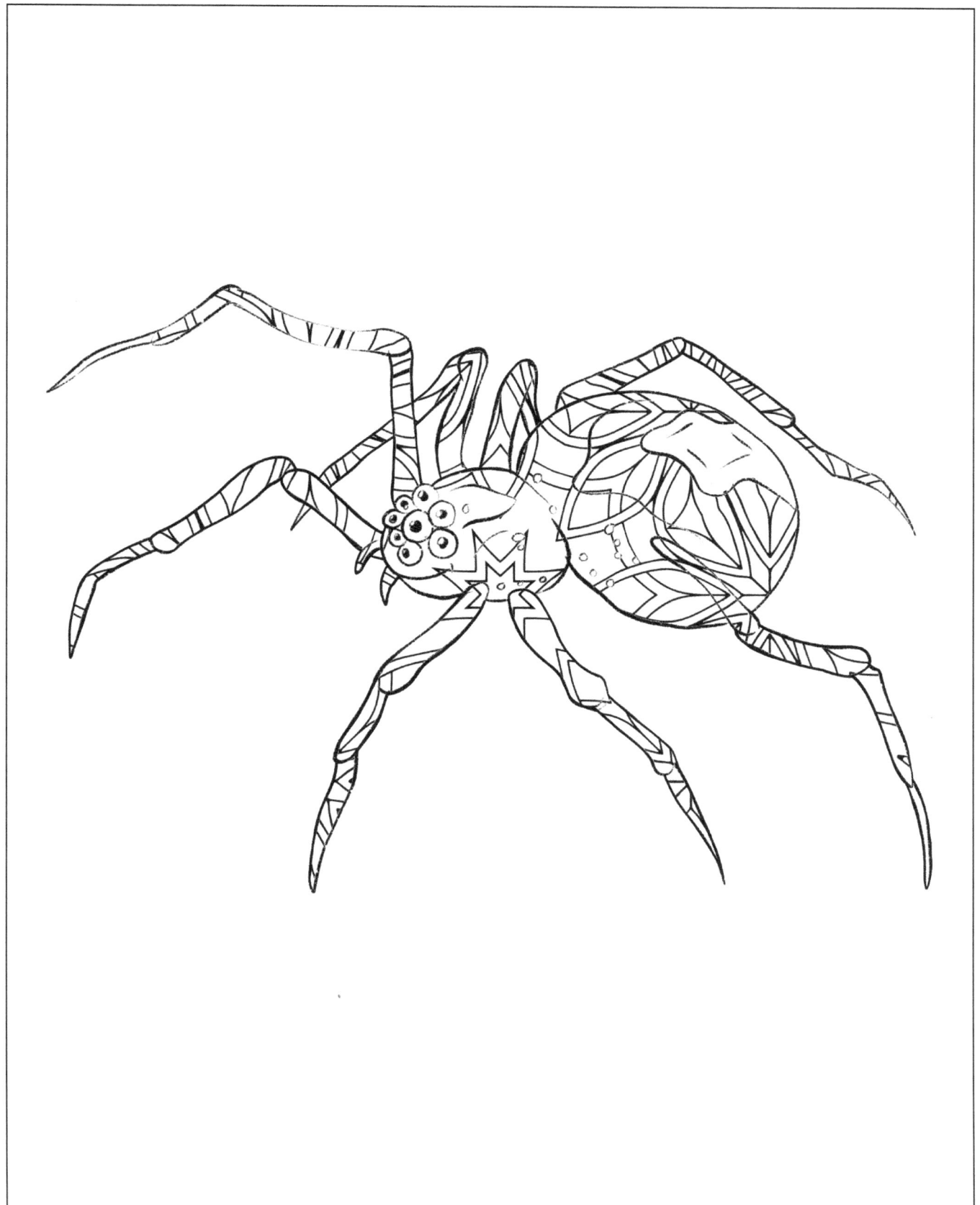

Black Widow

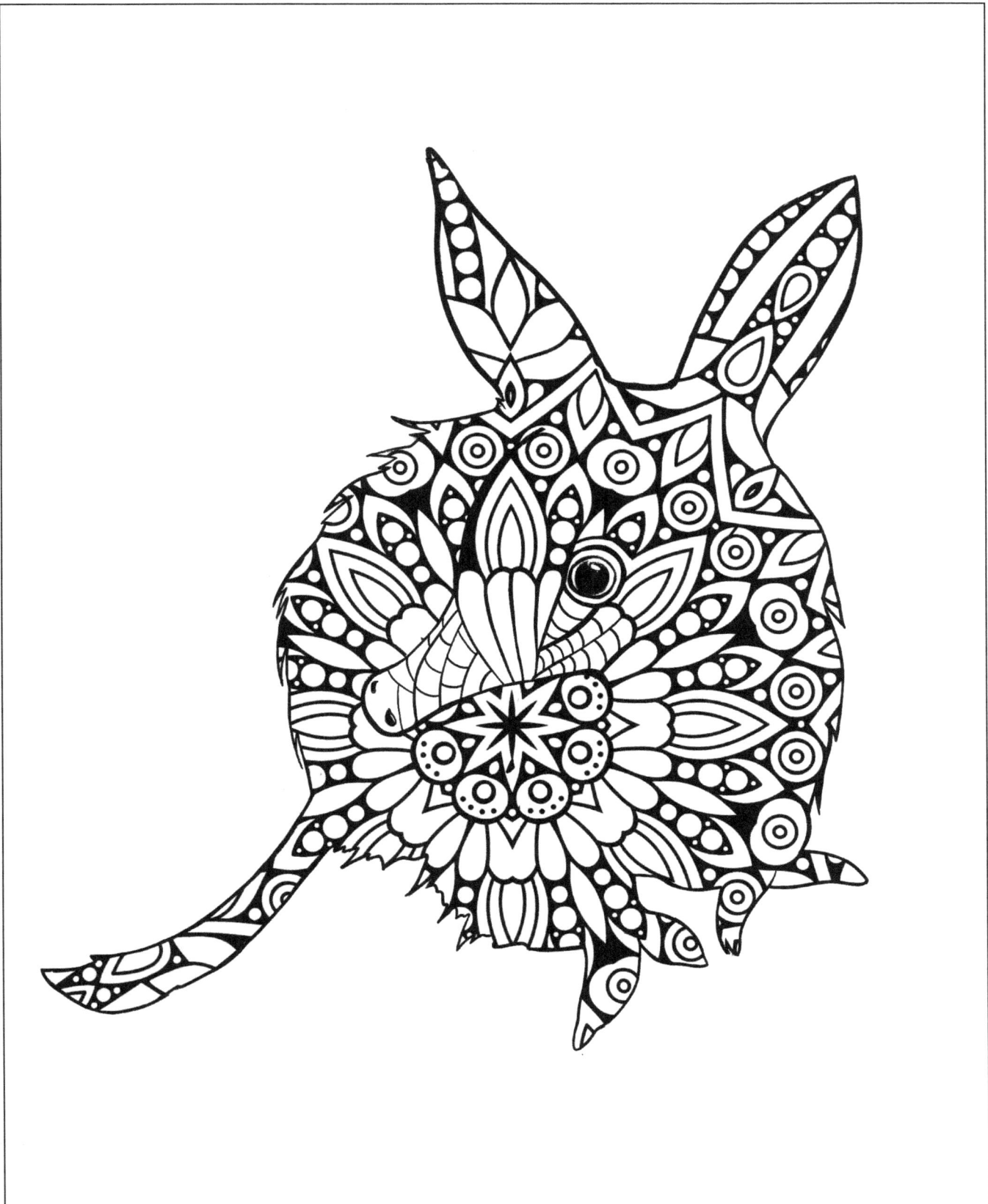

Bilby

www.ingramcontent.com/pod-product-compliance
Lightning Source LLC
Chambersburg PA
CBHW080437220526
45465CB00009B/3320